How Glass Beads Are Made

Preparation - Silica powder and soda ash are mixed with coloring agents.

Liquefaction - The mixture is melted in a kiln for about 20 hours at 1300°F.

Tube Making - In a kiln, glass is pulled into long thin shapes while air is blown into the center to form long tubes.

Cutting - The tubes are cut to approximate bead size by a blade spinning at extremely high speed.

First Baking - Cut pieces are placed in a 700°F rotating kiln to form round beads.

Cleaning - Beads are washed.

Finishing - Beads are heated in an electric kiln and polished to a high shine. Then various processes - coloring, lustre finishes, metallic finishes - are applied to the beads to enhance their beauty.

Features of Toho Beads

Large Holes - The size of the holes in Toho beads allows for threading multiple strands of thread or thicker thread, increasing the variety of beadwork you can achieve.

Light Weight - The larger hole means less weight so you get more beads when you buy by weight. There are approximately 111,800 size 11/0 Toho beads per kilo.

Toho Triangle Beads

Small & Large Round

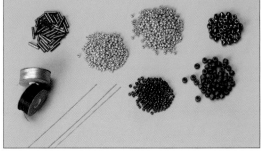

Basic Supplies: Toho Beads • Beading Needles • Beading Thread • Sharp Scissors

Beads to Wear... Every place, Everywhere and Every day!

Have fun making this free-flowing bracelet. The cubes slide along the bugles creating an ever-changing, fluid design!

Sliding Cubes Bracelets

Designed by Valarie Leland

Materials:
Gold/Bronze
3 grams 4 x 4 cube #22P
3 grams 8/0 #223
3 grams #3 Bugle #702

Silver/Black
3 grams 4 x 4 cube #21
3 grams 8/0 #610
3 grams #3 Bugle #610

Blue/Purple
3 grams 4 x 4 cube #22P
3 grams 8/0 #705
3 grams #3 Bugle #704

Basic Supplies:
Magnetic or snap clasp
Size 10 or 12 beading needle
Size D beading thread
Scissors

Start with a bit more than 2 yards of thread.

1. Pass the needle through the loop of the clasp and tie a knot.

2. Thread on 2 size 8/0 beads, 2 bugle beads and one cube. Make sure the cube slides easily over the bugles. If the cube will not slide, set it aside for another project.

3. Add an 8/0, 3 bugles and two cubes.

4. Repeat steps 2 and 3 until your bracelet is the correct length. You can randomly add two 8/0 beads between some of the bugle sets, if desired.

5. To attach the other end of the clasp, thread on two 8/0 beads after the last bugle. Pass through the clasp ring and go back down through only one of the 8/0 beads.

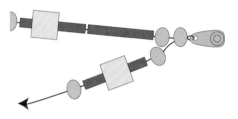

6. Pick up one 8/0 and repeat the first row instructions to make the second strand. To make the design more interesting, make sure the 8/0 beads separating the bugles do not line up on each strand.

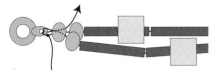

7. When you reach the opposite end, add one 8/0 and pass through the first 8/0 bead and the clasp loop. Go back down through the first 8/0 bead.

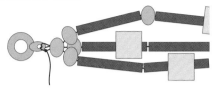

8. Repeat step 6 to make the third strand.

9. Pass the needle through the last 8/0 bead and the clasp. Thread needle back through the 8/0 bead and all the beads of the first row.

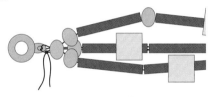

10. Tie the ends of thread together in a knot at the opposite end of the bracelet. Dot knot with glue to secure. Clip ends of thread.

Combine five different kinds of beads into a gracefully undulating ornament for your wrist!

Undulating Multi-Strand Bracelet

Designed by Valarie Leland

Materials:
Gold/Garnet
9 - 11 Garnet 6mm - 8mm fire polish beads or crystals
2 grams 11/0 #332 (color A)
3 grams 3.3 Treasures #332
3 grams 8/0 hex #22BF
2 grams 11/0 #2110 (color B)
2 Gold clamshell bead tips
Gold toggle clasp

Silver/Aqua
9 - 11 Aqua 6mm - 8mm fire polish beads or crystals
2 grams 11/0 #03 (color A)
3 grams 3.3 Treasures #21
3 grams 8/0 hex #163
2 grams 11/0 #551 (color B)
2 Silver clamshell bead tips
Silver toggle clasp

Gold/Amethyst
9 - 11 Amethyst 6mm - 8mm fire polish beads or crystals
2 grams 11/0 #205 (color A)
3 grams 3.3 Treasures #461
3 grams 8/0 hex #22BF
2 grams 11/0 #2110 (color B)
2 Gold clamshell bead tips
Gold toggle clasp

Basic Supplies:
Size 10 or 12 beading needle
C-lon or Nymo B beading thread
Scissors

Start with 48" of thread.

1. Thread on an 11/0 bead and tie the tail of thread in a knot around it. Pass needle through the slot in the clamshell tip. Do not close clamshell.

2. For the first strand, thread on five treasure beads and a fire polish bead. Repeat for a total of 9 fire polish beads. (7.5" bracelet)

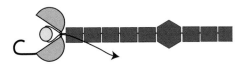

3. Add 5 more Treasures. Thread your needle through the slot in the second clamshell (this time in the opposite direction). Pick up an 11/0 and pass your needle back through the slot - the 11/0 will keep your thread from coming out of the clamshell.

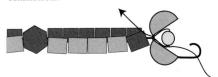

4. Pick up 5 hex beads and pass needle through the fire polish bead. Repeat to end. Pass your needle through the clamshell, the 11/0 and back through the clamshell again. Do not pull too tight, your bracelet will tighten up as you add strands.

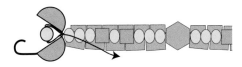

5. Pick up three 11/0 B, an 8 hex, an 11/0 B, an 8 hex and three 11/0 B then go through fire polish bead. Repeat to end. Go through the clamshell and the 11/0 stopper bead, then pass your needle back through the clamshell.

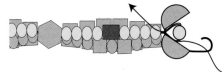

6. Pick up four 11/0 B, 3.3 Treasures and four 11/0 B then go through the fire polish bead. Repeat to end. Pass your needle through the clamshell, the 11/0 stopper bead and back through the clamshell.

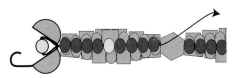

7. For the last row, pick up four 11/0 A, one 11/0 B and four 11/0 A then go through fire polish. Repeat to end.

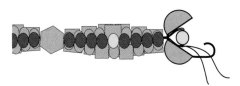

8. After going through the clamshell, the turning bead and the clamshell again, go back through the first row of Treasures and the clamshell at the other end.
Tie the threads together and add a drop of glue inside both clamshells. Cut the threads and close both clamshells.

9. Attach toggle clasp to clamshells.

ROUND SQUARES

Circle your arm with squares!
Make a bracelet with
cube and seed beads
in the colors of spring.
Using elastic to string
the last ring allows it to
slip on and off easily!

Designed by Valarie Leland

Materials:
Frosted Green & Pearl
5 grams 8/0 #121
22 grams 4mm cube #144F

Frosted Crystal & Blue
5 grams 8/0 #33F
22 grams 4mm cube #1F

Frosted Pink and Amethyst
5 grams 8/0 #39F
22 grams 4mm cube #145F

Basic Supplies:
Size 10 or 12 beading needle
Big-Eye of twisted wire needle
C-lon or Nymo B beading thread
6" of .5mm elastic thread
Scissors
Tape

Start with 36" of beading thread.
Thread needle with one end of thread.
Tape the opposite end to prevent the beads
from falling off.

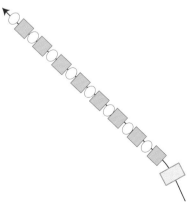

1. Pick up a cube, an 8/0, a cube, an 8/0 and repeat until you have 8 of each on the thread.

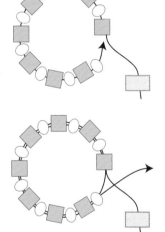

2. Make a ring by passing the needle back though all the beads in the same direction. Pull very tight so the ring is not loose or floppy.

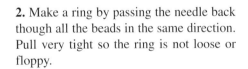

3. Both thread ends should be in the same space between beads. Tie a surgeon's knot. Push the needle through 4 to 6 beads next to the knot, pull tight and cut the thread. You may add a drop of glue or clear nail polish to the knot before you trim the tails.

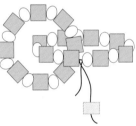

4. Thread on another series of cubes and 8/0s. Before you pass the needle back through all the beads, slip the first circle inside the new loop. Repeat step 3 to tie off and secure the new link.

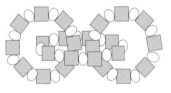

5. Join each new link to the chain as you did in step 4 until your bracelet is the desired length.

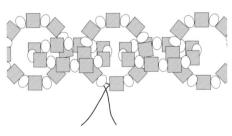

6. Make the final ring which connects the two ends of the bracelet with elastic thread. The ring will stretch and allow you to slip the bracelet on and off easily.

No climbing on this ladder...but success is sure to be yours when you bead this easy-to-make bracelet!

Ladder Bracelets

Designed by Valarie Leland

Materials:
Bronze/Garnet
3 grams 3.3 Treasures #332
5 grams 11/0 #2113
9 grams 4mm cube #22F

Silver/Green
3 grams 3.3 Treasures #601
5 grams 11/0 #284
9 grams 4mm cube #558

Gold/Crystal
3 grams 3.3 Treasures #21
5 grams 11/0 #551
9 grams 4mm cube #22F

Basic Supplies:
Size 10 or 12 beading needle
C-lon or Nymo B beading thread
Scissors

Start with 36" of thread.

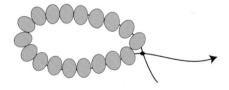

1. Pick up eighteen 11/0 beads and tie in a loop.

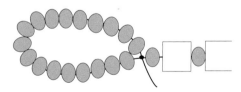

2. Pick up an 11/0, a cube and an 11/0 and repeat until you have 37 cube beads on the thread. (7.5" bracelet)

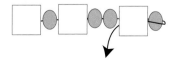

3. After the last cube, add two 11/0 beads, then pick up a cube and and 11/0 for the first side of the toggle. Pass the needle back down through the cube only. Leave a bit of slack in the thread below the toggle, about the width of two 11/0 beads. The space will keep your bracelet from kinking when you work the ladder between the sides.

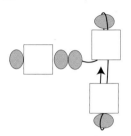

4. Pick up another cube and an 11/0. Pass the needle back through the cube.

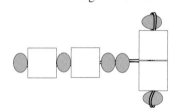

5. Pass the needle back through the first cube and the 11/0 on the other end. Pull tight but do not remove the slack.

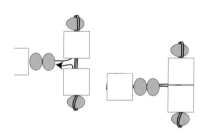

6. Pass the needle back through the toggle once more so that both ends of the toggle have two passes of thread through them. Come out between the cubes and go down through the two 11/0 beads and the first cube in the ladder and then carefully go through the beads all the way to the other end.

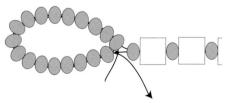

7. Pass back through the beginning loop of beads Tie a knot with the thread and the beginning tail. Dot the knot with glue to secure and clip the tails close.

8. Repeat steps 1 - 7 to make the other side of the ladder.

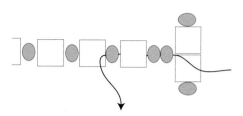

9. Thread the needle with 48" of thread. Pass through the two 11/0 beads under the toggle on one side. You will not need a stop bead, just wrap the end of the thread around your little finger or put a piece of tape on it. Come out of the 11/0 between the first 2 cube beads.

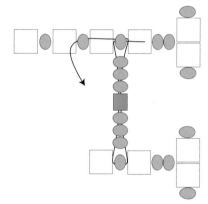

10. Pick up three 11/0, a Treasure and 3 more 11/0. Pass the needle through the 11/0 on the other side of the ladder. Bring your needle back up through all the beads. Pass your needle back through the original 11/0 bead and the next cube in the ladder. Bring your needle out after the next 11/0 in the row.

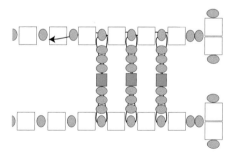

11. Repeat until all 11/0 beads between the cubes have a row of beads between them. Remember, you will always come out through an 11/0 and go into an 11/0 at the opposite side.

12. When you reach the opposite side, pass the thread back through one of the loops and weave back through a few stitches before trimming the tail. Weave the beginning tail through a few stitches. Trim close.

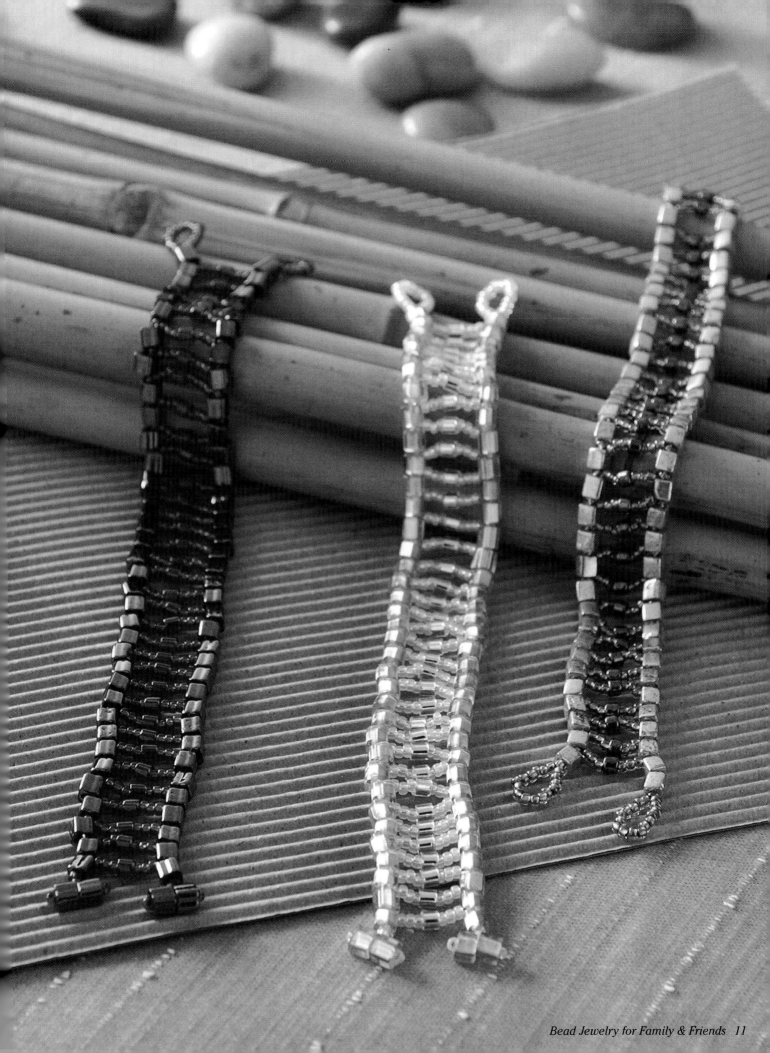

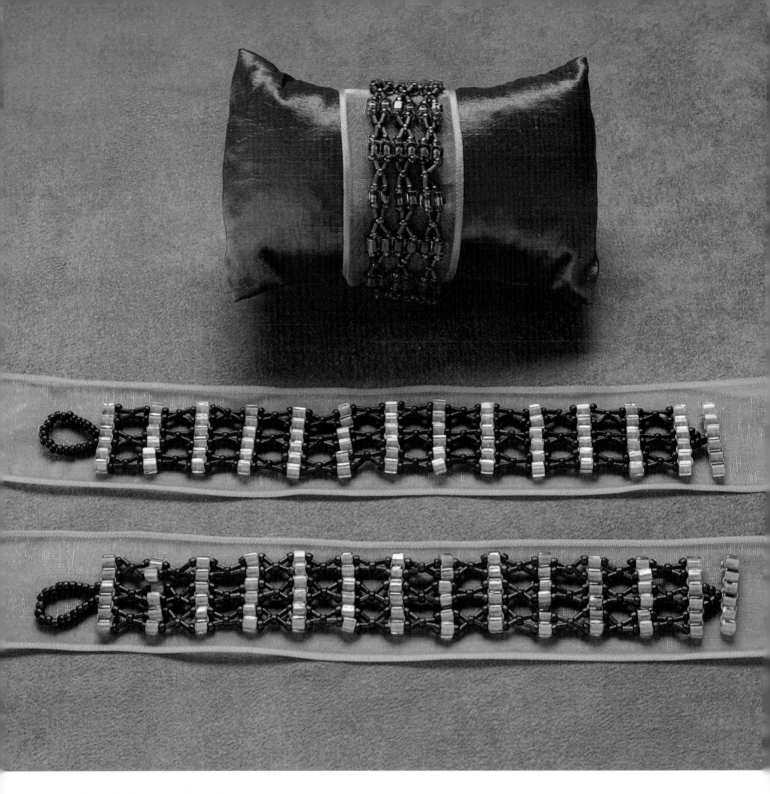

A lovely lattice of cube,
seed and bugle beads
TO GRACE ANY WRIST!

CRISS-CROSS
BRACELET

Designed by Valarie Leland

Materials:
Peony/Purple
2 grams #1 bugle #704
5 grams 8/0 #704
15 grams 4mm cube #943

Teal/Peacock
2 grams #1 bugle #705
5 grams 8/0 #705
15 grams 4mm cube #954

Lavender/Lilac
2 grams #1 bugle #87F
5 grams 8/0 #166D
15 grams 4mm cube #966

Basic Supplies:
Size 10 or 12 beading needle
C-lon or Nymo B beading thread
Scissors
Glue or clear nail polish, toothpick

Start with a 24" piece of thread.

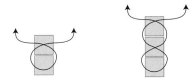

Make the stacks. Thread both ends with needles and place a cube at the center. Pick up a cube with one needle and go through that cube in the opposite direction with the other needle. Add four more cubes this way for a total of 6 cubes.

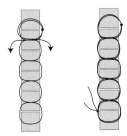

Tie the ends in a knot but don't clip the threads. Pass them back through the stack of cubes in a figure eight pattern just as before. Tie the threads again. Dot the knot with glue or clear nail polish to secure. Clip threads.
Repeat this process to make a total of 14 stacks.

Stop bead. Cut a 36" length of thread and pass through a bead twice in the same direction. This is called a stop bead.

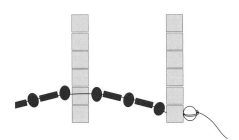

Row 1. Pass the thread through the first bead on one of the stacks.
Pick up an 8/0, bugle, 8/0, bugle, 8/0. Go through the second bead on one of the stacks. Pick up an 8/0, bugle, 8/0, bugle, 8/0. Go through the first bead on one of the stacks.
Repeat step 3 until you have connected 13 of the stacks - the 14th stack is the toggle bar for the closure and will be used later.

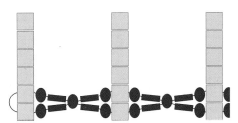

At the end of the row, pass the needle up through the second cube in the stack.
Row 2. Thread on an 8/0, and a bugle, pass the needle through the center 8/0 of Row 1. Thread on a bugle and an 8/0 and pass the needle through the first cube of the next stack. Thread on an 8/0, and a bugle, pass the needle through the center 8/0 of Row 1. Thread on a bugle and an 8/0 and pass the needle through the second cube of the next stack. Follow this beading pattern to complete the first row.

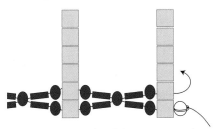

Row 3. At the end of the row, pass the needle up through the next cube in the stack and bead as for Row 1.

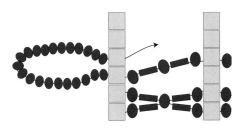

Loop and Row 4. When you get to the end of Row 3, thread on 22 11/0 beads to form the loop for the toggle. Pass through the fourth cube in the stack.
Before beginning the next row, pass needle back through the loop a few times to strengthen, then bead the row as you did in Row 2.

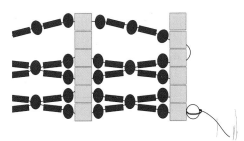

Row 5. At the end of Row 4, pass the needle through the next bead in the stack and bead this row as you did for Row 1.

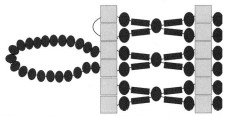

Row 6. Pass the needle through the next bead in the stack and bead the last row as you did for Row 2.

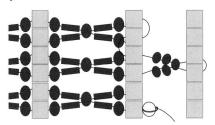

Toggle bar. Weave down as shown to reach the center two beads of the end stack. Thread on three 11/0 beads, pass through the toggle bar at the fourth bead and back through the third. Pass the needle through the first 11/0 and thread on two more 11/0 beads. Pass the needle through the third bead on the end stack. Make several passes through these beads to add strength.

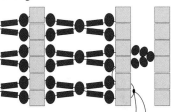

Remove the stopper bead. Weave the thread down one cube and tie ends to secure. Dot with glue. Clip ends.

Seed beads and tiny bugle beads are woven into a delicate net sure to catch compliments from all who see it!

Bugle Squares Bracelet

Designed by Valarie Leland

Materials:
Pearl
5 grams 11/0 #123
5 grams #1 Bugle #123

Red
5 grams 11/0 #25C
5 grams #1 Bugle #25C

Grey
5 grams 11/0 #704
5 grams #1 Bugle #704

Basic Supplies:
Three-strand slide bracelet clasp
Two size 10 or 12 beading needles
C-lon or Nymo B beading thread
Scissors
Cosmetic sponge, optional

Notes: Work the center row first, using 2 needles. Then use one needle to complete each side and add the clasp. These instructions are for a 7.5" bracelet. Each row adds approximately one half inch to the length. Smaller adjustments can be made during attachment of the clasp.
A cosmetic sponge is handy to wrap the thread around and hold one needle while you use the other.

Start with 90" of thread. Thread a needle on each side about 20" from the end.

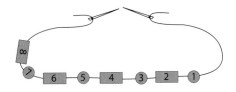

1. Pick up an 11/0, bugle, 11/0, bugle 11/0, bugle, 11/0, bugle. Slide them to the center of the thread.

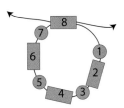

2. Pass the second needle in the opposite direction through the last bugle This is 'crossing the needles' through a bead. Pull to make a square and slide it to the center of the thread.

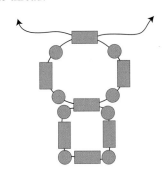

3. Pick up an 11/0, bugle,11/0 and bugle on the left needle. On the right needle pick up an 11/0, bugle and 11/0. Cross needles through the last bugle on the left side and pull snug. You now have 2 squares.
4. Repeat step 3 until you have a total of 28 squares.
5. Wrap the left needle and thread around a sponge or fold it inside a sticky note to keep it out of the way. Do not worry if the thread gets a little slack.

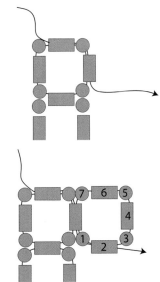

6. Pass the needle along the right side of the last square through the 11/0 and the bugle.
7. Pick up 11/0, bugle, 11/0, bugle, 11/0, bugle and 11/0 (beads 1 through 7).
Pass the needle down through the bugle on the center row and then through beads 1 and 2 of the current square.

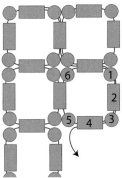

8. Pick up 11/0, bugle, 11/0, bugle and 11/0 (beads 1 through 5). Go up through the bugle on the center row. Pick up an 11/0 (6) and go through the bugle on the square above this new one. Pass through beads 1 through 4 to get to the bottom of this new square.

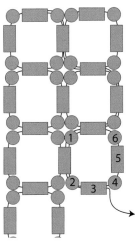

9. Pick up an 11/0 (1) and pass the needle down through the bugle on the center row. Pick up an 11/0, bugle, 11/0, bugle and 11/0 (beads 2 through 6). Go through the bugle on the bottom of the square above this one and back through bead 1, the center bugle and beads 2 and 3.

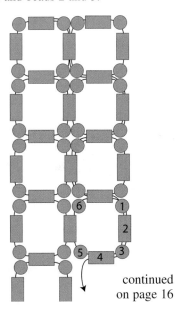

continued on page 16

10. Pick up 11/0, bugle, 11/0, bugle, 11/0, bugle (beads 1 through 5).

Pass the needle up through the bugle on the center row. Pick up an 11/0 (6) and go through the bugle on the bottom of the square above this one and then pass the needle through beads 1 though 4.

11. Repeat steps 8 and 9 until you have worked the length of the bracelet. Be sure not to take a 'shortcut' across a space with the thread. Always work around the squares to get your needle in position for the next stitch.

12. When you reach the opposite end of the bracelet, unwrap the left needle and wrap the right needle.

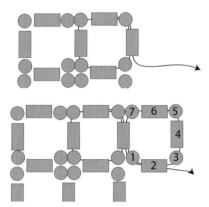

13. Flip your bracelet over and repeat steps 6 through 11 to complete the remaining row.

16. Pick up five 11/0 beads, thread the needle through the center loop of the clasp from front to back and then back through the bugle. Pass the needle back through these beads to reinforce.

17. Work the needle and thread around through the squares as shown to get to the last row.

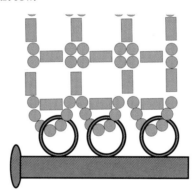

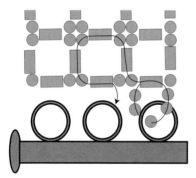

14. Pick up five 11/0 beads, thread the needle through the end loop of the clasp from back to front, then back through the bugle. Pass the needle back through these beads to reinforce.

15. Work the needle and thread through the squares as shown to the center row.

18. Pick up five 11/0 beads, thread the needle through the end loop of the clasp from back to front and then back through the bugle. Pass the needle back through these beads to reinforce.

19. Work the needle through 2 or 3 of the squares toward the center of the bracelet and cut the thread close.

20. Unwrap the other needle and add the clasp by repeating steps 14 - 19. Make sure you have the clasp facing the correct way.

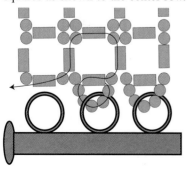

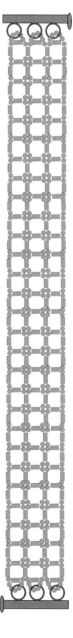

Circle ‚ Circle ‚ Circle
Bracelets & Earrings

Don't go around in circles searching
for the perfect project... try your hand
at this lovely jewelry of beaded disks!

Designed by Marilou Porth

Materials:
Bronze/Red
2.5 grams 1.8 Treasures #221
2.5 grams 1.8 Treasures #798

Copper
2.5 grams 1.8 Treasures #222 (rows 5-7)
2.5 grams 1.8 Treasures #703 (rows 1-4)

Gold
2.5 grams 1.8 Treasures #949
2.5 grams 1.8 Treasures #712

Basic Supplies:
Nylon snap
Pair of ear wires
Size 10 or 12 beading needle
C-lon or Nymo D beading thread
Scissors

continued on page 18

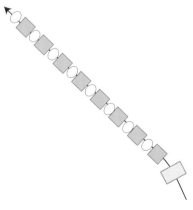

1. Pick up a cube, an 8/0, a cube, an 8/0 and repeat until you have 8 of each on the thread.

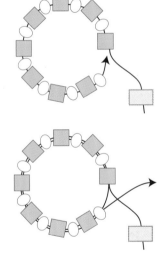

2. Make a ring by passing the needle back though all the beads in the same direction. Pull very tight so the ring is not loose or floppy.

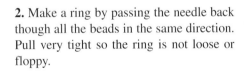

3. Both thread ends should be in the same space between beads. Tie a surgeon's knot. Push the needle through 4 to 6 beads next to the knot, pull tight and cut the thread. You may add a drop of glue or clear nail polish to the knot before you trim the tails.

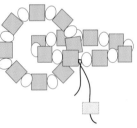

4. Thread on another series of cubes and 8/0s. Before you pass the needle back through all the beads, slip the first circle inside the new loop. Repeat step 3 to tie off and secure the new link.

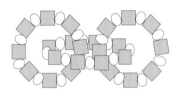

5. Join each new link to the chain as you did in step 4 until your bracelet is the desired length.

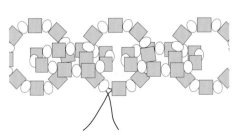

6. Make the final ring which connects the two ends of the bracelet with elastic thread. The ring will stretch and allow you to slip the bracelet on and off easily.

No climbing on this ladder...but success is sure to be yours when you bead this easy-to-make bracelet!

Ladder Bracelets

Designed by Valarie Leland

Materials:
Bronze/Garnet
3 grams 3.3 Treasures #332
5 grams 11/0 #2113
9 grams 4mm cube #22F

Silver/Green
3 grams 3.3 Treasures #601
5 grams 11/0 #284
9 grams 4mm cube #558

Gold/Crystal
3 grams 3.3 Treasures #21
5 grams 11/0 #551
9 grams 4mm cube #22F

Basic Supplies:
Size 10 or 12 beading needle
C-lon or Nymo B beading thread
Scissors

Start with 36" of thread.

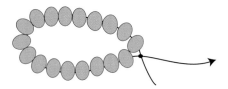

1. Pick up eighteen 11/0 beads and tie in a loop.

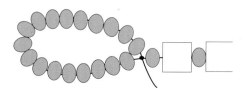

2. Pick up an 11/0, a cube and an 11/0 and repeat until you have 37 cube beads on the thread. (7.5" bracelet)

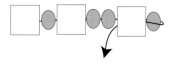

3. After the last cube, add two 11/0 beads, then pick up a cube and and 11/0 for the first side of the toggle. Pass the needle back down through the cube only. Leave a bit of slack in the thread below the toggle, about the width of two 11/0 beads. The space will keep your bracelet from kinking when you work the ladder between the sides.

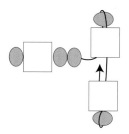

4. Pick up another cube and an 11/0. Pass the needle back through the cube.

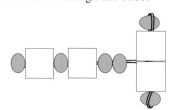

5. Pass the needle back through the first cube and the 11/0 on the other end. Pull tight but do not remove the slack.

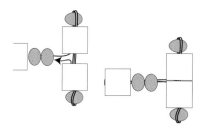

6. Pass the needle back through the toggle once more so that both ends of the toggle have two passes of thread through them. Come out between the cubes and go down through the two 11/0 beads and the first cube in the ladder and then carefully go through the beads all the way to the other end.

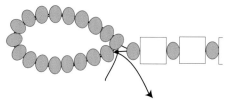

7. Pass back through the beginning loop of beads Tie a knot with the thread and the beginning tail. Dot the knot with glue to secure and clip the tails close.

8. Repeat steps 1 - 7 to make the other side of the ladder.

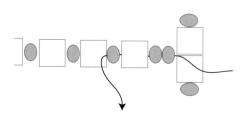

9. Thread the needle with 48" of thread. Pass through the two 11/0 beads under the toggle on one side. You will not need a stop bead, just wrap the end of the thread around your little finger or put a piece of tape on it. Come out of the 11/0 between the first 2 cube beads.

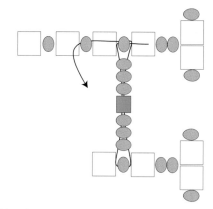

10. Pick up three 11/0, a Treasure and 3 more 11/0. Pass the needle through the 11/0 on the other side of the ladder. Bring your needle back up through all the beads. Pass your needle back through the original 11/0 bead and the next cube in the ladder. Bring your needle out after the next 11/0 in the row.

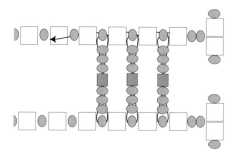

11. Repeat until all 11/0 beads between the cubes have a row of beads between them. Remember, you will always come out through an 11/0 and go into an 11/0 at the opposite side.

12. When you reach the opposite side, pass the thread back through one of the loops and weave back through a few stitches before trimming the tail. Weave the beginning tail through a few stitches. Trim close.

Row 1. (3 beads) Using a comfortable length of thread, pick up 3 beads and pull them about 8" from the end of your thread. Pass the needle through the first bead and pull the beads into a circle.

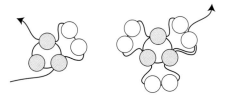

Row 2. (6 beads) Place 2 beads in between each bead from Row 1. Be sure to hold your tension tight. Step up to start the next row by passing needle through the first bead in the row you just finished. Your needle will be coming out between the first pair of beads added.

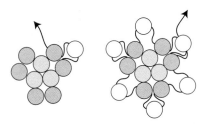

Row 3. (6 beads) Add one bead between the pairs of beads and one bead in the spaces At this point you will need to step up to the next row.

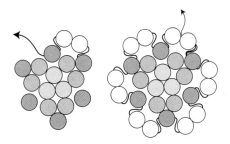

Row 4. (12 beads) Place 2 beads in each space. Step up at the end of the row. The needle will be coming out between the first pair of beads added.

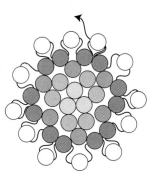

Row 5. (12 beads) Place one bead between each pair of beads and in each space. Step up at end of row.

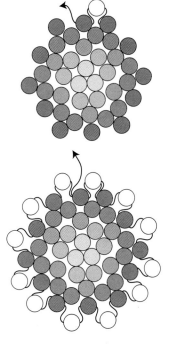

Row 6. (12 beads) Place one bead in each space. Do **not** step up at the end of the row.

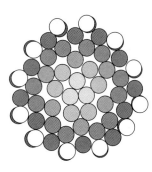

Row 7. (12 beads) Row 7 is a duplicate of Row 6. Stitch one bead between each of the beads from Row 5. Row 7 will push the beads from Row 6 off center and form a ridge.

Weave the needle back through several rows of stitching to secure before clipping thread ends.

Earrings.

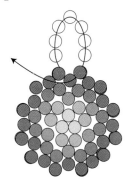

Make the ear wire loop: Create 2 circle elements for each earring. With the needle coming out of a bead from Row 5, thread on 5 to 7 beads and create a loop for the ear wire by passing the needle back through the opposite side of the same bead on Row 5.

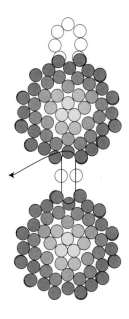

Connect the circles: Pass needle through the beads along the thread path until needle comes out of the Row 5 bead directly opposite the hanging loop. Pick up a bead, pass through a bead from Row 5 of the other circle and pick up a bead. Pass needle through the bead in Row 5 of the first circle to complete the connecting loop.

Bracelet. Create 2 circle elements for every inch of desired finished length plus one element for the clasp. For a 7" bracelet you will need 15 circle elements. Join elements following earring instructions. Stitch a nylon snap to the underside of one end and to the upper side of the other end.

Jeweled Collar Necklace

Designed by Marilou Porth

If glamour is your goal, this is the perfect project for you! Triangle, seed and teardrop beads create a look of luxury!

Basic Supplies:
Shank button to match beads
Size 10 or 12 beading needle
Power-pro or Fireline thread
Scissors

Materials:

Pearl
10 grams 8/0 triangle #161
5 grams 8/0 #121
30 grams 11/0 #121
70 to 80 top-drilled freshwater pearls
Pearl button

Green and Bronze
10 grams 8/0 triangle #84F
5 grams 8/0 #221
30 grams 3-cut #221
70 to 80 emerald Austrian crystals

Iridescent Grey
10 grams 8/0 triangle #86
5 grams 8/0 #566
30 grams 11/0 #176B
70 to 80 top-drilled iridescent grey pearls

Thread the needle with 60" of thread. Pick up a bead and pass through it twice in the same direction. Be careful not to split the thread. Leave a 12" tail. This is a stopper bead and it is there to prevent the working beads from coming off the end of the thread. You may have to move the stopper bead down the tail from time to time to make room for the working beads. Likewise, you might have to move it closer to the working beads to help you keep the proper tension.

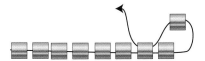

Rows 1 - 2. Using triangle beads, pick up 16" or desired length of beads. Make sure the number is divisible by 2. Pick up a bead, skip a bead and pass through a bead. Pick up a bead, skip a bead and pass through a bead.

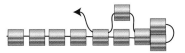

Complete the row by stitching the remaining beads in the same manner. Notice how the beads from the first row 'share' the space with the new beads.

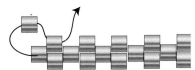

Row 3. Pick up a bead and pass the needle through the first high bead of the row.

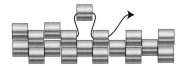

Place a bead in between each tall bead of the previous row.

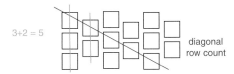

Rows 4 - 5. Continue to add beads in this manner until you have a total of 5 rows. Peyote stitch is counted on the diagonal. An easier way to count is to add 2 columns of beads.

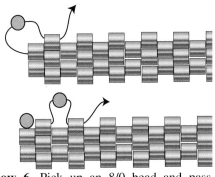

Row 6. Pick up an 8/0 bead and pass through the next tall triangle bead. Continue across the necklace. This final row is the one that causes the collar to curve and fit the neck. When you reach the other end of the peyote strip, pull your thread taut. Since the 8/0 beads are smaller than the triangle beads your work will curve in.

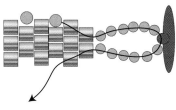

Attach button by picking up a few 11/0 beads, passing through shank of button, a few more 11/0 beads and back into the peyote strip. Pass through the beads and button several times to ensure a sturdy connection. Work your needle until it is coming out of a high bead on the bottom row of the peyote strip.

Jeweled Loops:
Pick up fourteen 11/0 beads, a teardrop or crystal and fifteen 11/0 beads. Pass through the same high bead on the oppo-

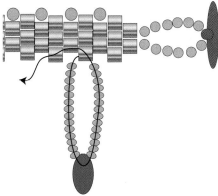

site side and weave through to the next high bead. Continue adding loops of fringe between the high beads.

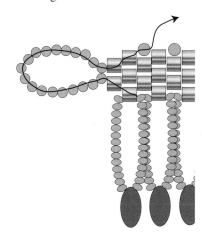

To finish this end of the collar, pick up enough seed beads to accommodate the button. Be sure to use an odd number. Pass through the beads several times to ensure a sturdy loop. Weave through several rows of stitching to secure before clipping ends.

Magic Lace Bracelet

Designed by Valarie Leland

Materials:

This exquisite bracelet
has just enough stretch
to slip over your hand
and hug your wrist!

Red
15 grams size 1 bugle #25CF
3 grams 11/0 #25 (colors A & B)
2 grams 15/0 #25C

Bronze
15 grams size 1 bugle #221
2 grams 11/0 #703 (color A)
1 gram 11/0 #221 (color B)
2 grams 15/0 #221

Purple
15 grams size 1 bugle #704
2 grams 11/0 #704 (color A)
1 gram 11/0 #327 (color B)
2 grams 15/0 #704

Basic Supplies:
Size 10 or 12 beading needle
C-lon or Nymo B beading thread
Beeswax
Scissors

Inspect the bugles and remove any that are obviously too long, too short or that have sharp ends.

To determine how long to make your bracelet, pretend that you are going to slide on a bangle bracelet with your fingers close together and your thumb over your palm and measure your hand at the widest part. That is the length of your bracelet when it is slightly stretched. You do not want it to be stretched to the max every time you put it on, it might break under the stress. If your hand measures 8", your bracelet should be about 6" long.

This length will fit closely on a 7" wrist.
1. Cut a double arm's length of thread. Pick up a bead and pass through it twice in the same direction. Be careful not to split the thread. Leave a 6" tail. This is a stopper bead and it is there to prevent the working beads from coming off the end of the thread. You may have to move the stopper bead down the tail from time to time to make room for the working beads. Likewise, you might have to move it closer to the working beads to help you keep the proper tension.

2. Alternate one A and one bugle until you have 9 bugles.

3. Add one A, one B and three 15/0 beads. Pass the needle back through the B and A beads and make a picot with three 15/0 beads on top of the A bead.

4. Add bugle, A and bugle. Skip bugle, A and bugle in the first row and pass the needle through the next A bead in the first row. Do not go through any of the bugles in the first row, only through a single A bead. These beads are shared between adjacent rows.

5. Add bugle, A and bugle. Skip bugle, A and bugle, go through the next A bead in the first row.

6. Repeat step 5 until there is only one bugle left 'unattached' in the first row.

Add one bugle to the current row.

7. Add A, B and three 15/0 beads. Pass the needle back through the B and A beads to add the picot.

So far you will have 2 rows of bugles and 11/0 beads lined up next to each other. Do not worry, by the sixth row they will start to expand into the diamond shape.
8. Repeat steps 4 through 7 keeping an even tension - not too tight.

Occasionally pull the ends in opposite directions to make the beads line up.

9. When your bracelet is the correct length, stop after step 7. Use the last row to weave both sides together and close the bracelet. The needle will be coming out through an A bead after the last picot.

Pick up a bugle. Pass the needle through the second A bead on the first row, the one that sticks out a bit like an elbow. Pick up another bugle and pass the needle through the A bead that is elbowing out the last row you worked.

10. Keep going from side to side - adding one bugle and going through A beads. When you get to the last bugle, it will be angling back toward the very first bugle and stop bead. Pass the needle through the A bead coming out next to the tail thread and stop bead. Remove the stop bead. Pick up a B bead and three 15/0 beads. Pass the needle back up through the B bead and tie a double knot with the 2 tails.

Pass the needle up through the A bead and through a row of the bugle and A beads. Do not try to take a shortcut, you should go all the way across the bracelet up into the picot and back down a few beads. Clip the thread. Thread the tail on the needle and weave it through a row of the bracelet in the other direction before clipping.

A simple
ladder stitch bracelet
is made extraordinary
with opulent fringe!

Fringe, Fringe, Fringe Bracelets

Designed by Marilou Porth

Materials:

Silver
5 grams 4mm cube #566
18 grams 1.8 Treasures #602 (colors A, B)
300 or more 4mm fire polish Silver AB

Green/Bronze
5 grams 4mm cube #221
3 grams 1.8 Treasures #507 (colors A, B)
15 grams 1.8 Treasures #710 (color C)
1 gram 1.8 Treasures #221
300 or more size 5 Triangle #221

Red/Bronze
5 grams 3.3 Treasures #332
3 grams 1.8 Treasures #221 (color A)
5 grams 1.8 Treasures #329 (color B)
1 grams 1.8 Treasures #241(color C)
300 or more 4mm round Bronze

Basic Supplies:
Shank button to match beads
Size 10 or 12 beading needle
C-lon or Nymo D beading thread
Beeswax, not Thread Heaven
Scissors

The bracelet base is worked in ladder stitch.

1. To start, thread the needle with about 6 feet of thread. Double the thread and wax it so it holds together. Pick up a bead and pass through it twice in the same direction. Be careful not to split the thread. Leave a 12" tail. This is a stopper bead and it is there to prevent the working beads from coming off the end of the thread.

You may have to move the stopper bead down the tail from time to time to make room for the working beads. Likewise, you might have to move it closer to the working beads to help you keep the proper tension.

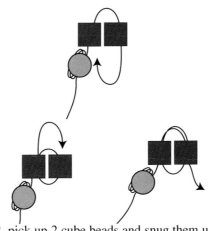

2. pick up 2 cube beads and snug them up to the the stop bead. Arrange the beads as shown above and pass your needle up through the first bead, then down through the second bead.

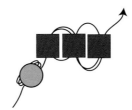

3. Pick up another cube bead. Arrange the beads as shown above. Pass your needle in a circle up through the new bead, back down through the last bead and back up through the new bead.

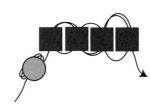

4. Pick up another cube bead. Arrange the beads as shown above. Pass your needle in a circle down through the new bead, up through the last bead and down through the new bead.
Repeat steps 3 & 4 until you reach the desired length about 1/2" shorter than finished length.

5. Attach button by picking up a few 11/0 beads, passing through shank of button, a few more 11/0 beads and back into the cube strip. Pass through the beads and button several times to ensure a sturdy connection.

Making the fringe. Each cube bead will have 3 fringes coming out of each side.
Long Fringe: 10 color A beads, one Accent bead, one color C bead.
Medium Fringe: 7 color B, one Accent, one color C.
Short Fringe: 3 color C, one Accent, one color C.

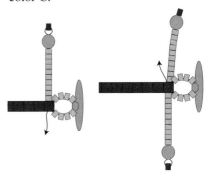

6. With the needle coming out of the last cube bead, pick up the beads for the long fringe. Pass needle back through all but the last bead creating a single fringe. You should be coming out of the other side of the cube. Repeat for another long fringe.

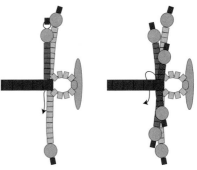

Continue in this manner working back and forth to make one long, one medium and one short fringe on each side of the cube bead. Continue until you have fringed all the cube beads

7. To finish the other end of the bracelet, pick up enough seed beads to accommodate the button. Be sure to use an odd number. Pass through the beads several time to ensure a sturdy loop.

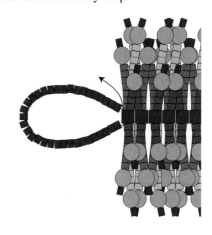

Elegant Spiral Bracelet

Designed by Valarie Leland

Materials:

Shamrock
4 grams 11 hex #270
4 grams 8 hex Bugle #167B
4 grams 8/0 #22BF
Four 4mm emerald fire polish beads
Two 6mm emerald fire polish beads

Lilac
4 grams 11 hex #85
4 grams 8 hex Bugle #202
4 grams 8/0 #554F
Four 4mm purple AB fire polish beads
Two 6mm purple AB fire polish beads

Rose
4 grams 11 hex #329
4 grams 8 hex Bugle #365
4 grams 8/0 #221
Four 4mm gold/rose fire polish beads
Two 6mm gold/rose fire polish beads

Basic Supplies:
Size 10 or 12 beading needle
C-lon or Nymo B beading thread
Scissors

Thread 48" of thread on a needle.

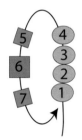

1. Pick up four 8/0 beads, 11 hex, 8 hex and 11 hex. Pass the needle again the same way through the four 8/0 beads. Move this group of beads to the right side of your work. Hold onto an 8" tail of thread. After the first 3 groups, the beads will remain in place.

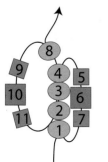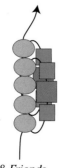

2. Pick up another 8/0, 11 hex, 8 hex and 11 hex and slide them down the thread to the end. Skip the first 8/0 bead and pass needle through the second through fourth beads and then the 8/0 you just added. Keep the new hex beads from overlapping the first set, but push them to the back next to the first set and pull snug. You can work the spiral right-handed or left-handed, just be sure to always push the new hex beads over the same way each time.

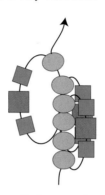

3. Repeat step 3 always going through the last three 8/0 core beads in the stack and the new one added until your bracelet is the desired length.

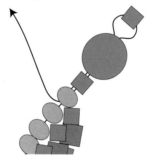

4. The thread will be coming out from the 8/0 core beads. Add 11 hex, 6mm fire polish and another 11 hex. Pass the needle back through the fire polish and first hex bead, and through the last 8/0 core bead. This group of beads will be the clasp that will go through a loop on the opposite end.

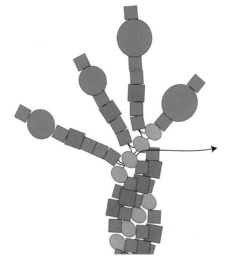

5. Add a row of bead fringe between the next 3 core beads. After the third group, pass the needle back through the third core bead in the opposite direction and add a second row of fringe between the last two core beads Use four to six 11 hex beads and include an 8 hex at different spots on each dangle. Top them with the second 6mm and 4mm fire polish beads. Do not let the tension get too tight or the bracelet

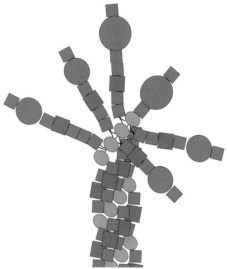

will be spiky and stiff looking.
6. Go back through the clasp beads to reinforce then work your way down the core and through the hex beads to lock the thread in place. Trim thread close to beads.
7. Check the final length of your bracelet. If it is too short, you can add to the starting end before making the loop. If it is too long, carefully remove stitches.

8. Thread the needle with the tail thread at the other end of the bracelet. Pick up fifteen 11 hex beads. Run the needle back into the core and come out through the 5th bead.
Pass the needle around the second loop of the spiral, up through the last core bead and back through the closing loop. Pass the needle back through several loops of the spiral before clipping the thread end.

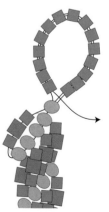

Cinch your wrist with
an elegant rope of jewel toned
hex and fire polish beads!

LEARN TO MAKE zip beads
AND YOU CAN HAVE AN
AMAZING VARIETY OF beads
ANY TIME. EACH PROJECT
will be TRULY UNIQUE!

MORE ZIP BEADS

Designed by Marilou Porth

Materials:
Less than 1 gram of 1 to 3 colors
of 1.8 treasures are needed for each bead

Basic Supplies:
Toggle clasp
Bali 5mm or 6mm daisy spacers
Silver 4mm beads
4mm Austrian crystal bicones
Size 10 or 12 beading needle
C-lon or Nymo D beading thread
12" of .015 flexible beading wire
2 crimp tubes or beads
Ear wires
Head pins

Each of the embellished beads is made over a peyote tube base. There are two types of base bead. One made with an even number of beads and another made with an odd number.

Thread the needle with 36" of thread. Pick up a bead and pass through it twice in the same direction. Be careful not to split the thread. Leave a 12" tail. This is a stopper bead and it is there to prevent the working beads from coming off the end of the thread. You may have to move the stopper bead down the tail from time to time to make room for the working beads. Likewise, you might have to move it closer to the working beads to help you keep the proper tension.

Even Count Base
Rows 1 & 2:

String an even number of treasure beads. Thread on another bead. Skip over one bead and pass the needle through the second bead in the row.

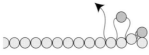

Thread on another bead. Skip over a bead and pass the needle through the next bead in the row.

Complete row by stitching the remaining beads in the same manner.
Notice how the beads from the first row "share" the space with the new beads?

Row 3:
Reverse direction. Thread on a bead and pass the needle through the first "tall" bead of the row.

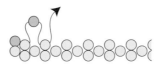

Add a bead between each of the "tall" beads of the row.
Rows 4 - 10:
Continue to add beads in this manner until you have a total of 10 rows.

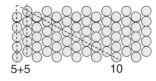

5+5   10

Peyote stitch is counted on the diagonal. An easier way to count is to add 2 columns. Both methods are shown above.

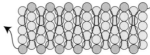

Fold the ends together and you'll notice that they fit together like the teeth of a zipper. Stitch the two ends together.
Weave the ends of your thread through the beaded piece until they are secure. Clip the ends close.

Odd Count Base
Rows 1 & 2:

String an odd number of treasure beads.

Thread on another bead. Skip over one bead and pass the needle through the second bead in the row.

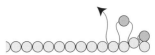

Thread on another bead. Skip over a bead and pass the needle through the next bead in the row.
Complete the row by stitching the remaining beads.

Pass the needle through the last two beads of the row. Add a bead and then make a figure eight pattern as shown.
Row 3:

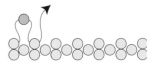

Reverse direction. Thread on a bead and pass the needle through the next "tall" bead of the row. Add a bead between each of the "tall" beads of the row.
Row 4 :

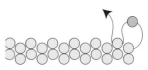

Reverse direction and add beads between each of the tall beads of the row as shown.
Rows 5 - 10:
Repeat Rows 3 and 4 until you have a total of 10 rows. Peyote stitch is counted on the diagonal. An easier way to count is to add 2 columns. Both methods are shown at left.
Fold the ends together and you'll notice that they fit together like the teeth of a zipper. Stitch the two ends together as shown at left. Weave the ends of your thread through the beaded piece until they are secure. Clip the ends close.

continued on pages 30 - 31

More Zip Beads... continued from pages 28 - 29

Polka Dot Bead - Odd Count

1. Begin with an odd count tube bead of 11 beads and 10 rows. Pass the needle through two of the outside beads of the tube.

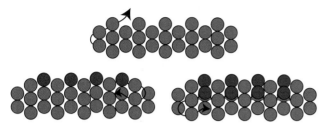

2. Peyote stitch 4 beads. Bring the needle back through the next bead in the vertical row and peyote stitch 4 more beads. Bring the needle back through the next bead in the vertical row. Continue to peyote stitch the four center beads of every other row until you have added 5 rows of beads.

3. Weave the needle back through several rows of stitching before clipping ends close.

Layered Bead - Even Count

1. Begin with an even count tube bead of 10 beads and 10 rows.

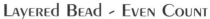

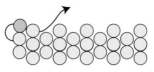

2. Pass the needle through two of the outside beads of the tube. Peyote stitch 1 bead.

3. Reverse direction and work even count flat peyote out from the tube for 22 rows.

4. Wrap the flat peyote piece around the tube. Join the ends as you did for the original tube.

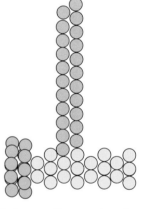

5. Work the needle over two beads and peyote stitch one bead of even count flat peyote for 22 rows.

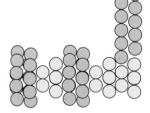

6. Wrap and join.

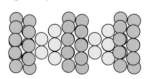

7. Repeat the process for the last two beads of the row.

Melon Bead

This bead starts off as an odd count peyote tube which is then embellished with 6 wings creating a melon appearance.

1. Make an odd count tube 11 beads wide and 12 rows long.

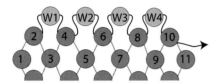

2. Work the needle until it is coming out of base bead 2. Peyote stitch 4 beads. You will be coming out of bead 10.

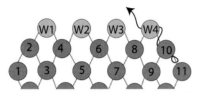

3. Pass needle under the thread between beads 10 and 11 and pass back through beads 10 and wing bead 4.

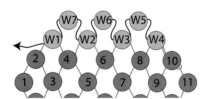

4. Peyote stitch 3 beads. You will be coming out of wing bead 1.

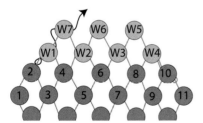

5. Pass needle under the thread between wing bead 1 and base bead 2. Pass back through wing beads 1 and 7.

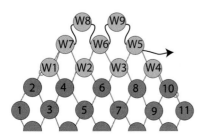

6. Peyote stitch 2 beads. You will be coming out of wing bead 5.

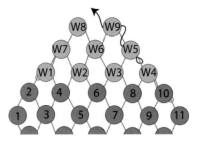

7. Pass needle under the thread between wing beads 5 and 4. Pass back through wing beads 5 and 9.

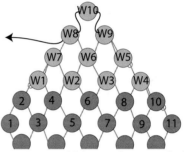

8. Peyote stitch 1 bead. You will be coming out of wing bead 8.

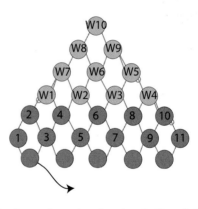

9. Pass needle down through wing beads 7 and 1, and base beads 2 and 1. Turn and pass needle through the next end bead adjacent to bead 1 (bead A2). Repeat the instructions for wing #1.

Repeat the process to stitch a total of 6 wings.

Variation: Make the base bead 7 beads wide and 10 rows long. Wings will start with a base of 3 beads and there will be only 5 wings.

continued on pages 32 - 33

More Zip Beads... continued from pages 30 - 31

Diamond Bead

This bead starts off as an odd count peyote tube. Two pair of wings are added adjacent to each other. Each pair share the top 3 beads which pulls the wings and the beads flat creating a diamond shape. Make an odd count tube bead in one color 11 beads wide and 12 rows long.

Gently press and smooth the bead until it is flattened.

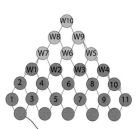

Wing 1: Work as for melon bead (page 31). Follow beading pattern above.

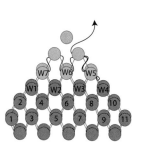

Wing 2: Repeat the instructions for wing #1 *except* use wing beads 8, 9 and 10 from wing #1 to complete wing #2.

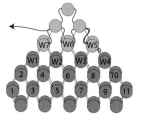

Repeat the process to stitch wing #3 and #4 on the opposite side of the bead.

Picot Bead - Even Count

Begin with an even count tube bead of 10 beads and 8 rows.

If you look at the bead closely, you can plainly see the rows of beads.

Begin with the thread coming out of a bead at the end of the tube. Thread on a color A, color B and color A treasure bead.

Bring the needle up through the bead just below and to the right of the end bead.

Thread on another set of ABA beads. Bring the needle up through the bead just below and to the right of the bead you just exited. Repeat this process around the length of the bead.

Variation: Make two rows of picots around the bead.

How to Make a Bracelet

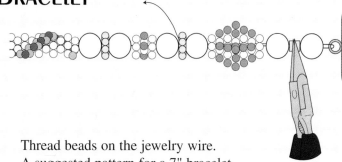

Thread one end of the wire through a crimp tube, a silver bead and the loop of an earring (see page 33 for instructions). Pass the wire through one end of the toggle clasp and then back through the silver bead and the crimp bead. Flatten the crimp with chain-nose pliers.

Thread beads on the jewelry wire. A suggested pattern for a 7" bracelet is shown above.

Thread another crimp bead and a silver bead on the remaining end of jewelry wire. Pass the wire through the other half of the toggle clasp and then back through both beads. Flatten the crimp bead with chain-nose pliers.

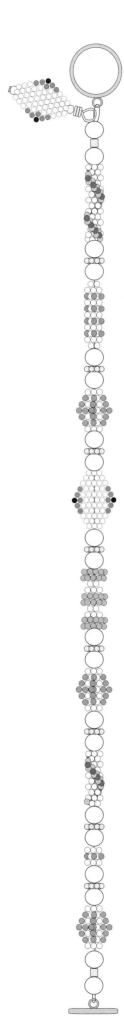

How to Make Earrings

1. Thread a silver bead, a zip bead and another silver bead on a 3" head pin.

2. Grasp the pin with your pliers about $1/8$" from the end of the jaws.

3. The pliers should be touching the top of the silver bead.

Bend the wire at a 90° angle.

Pivot the pliers from horizontal to vertical.

4. Wrap the wire around the top jaw of the pliers.

Reposition the wire on the bottom jaw of the pliers.

Wrap the wire around the bottom jaw of the pliers as shown.

5. Grasp the loop of the dangle with the pliers. Without touching the beads on the head pin, begin coiling the short end around the neck of the dangle.

6. Begin the coils as close to the loop as possible. Make two or three coils, then clip the end of the wire close to the coils.

Open the loop on the ear wire and thread on the earring. Close the ear wire loop. Repeat for the remaining earring.

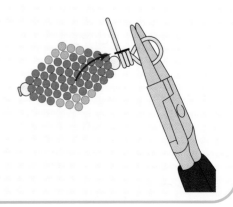